He Chose the

GLORY

The Life and Legacy of Obed-Edom

He Chose the

GLORY

The Life and Legacy of Obed-Edom

"This entire unique book will grip you...."
—Mark Batterson

Louis McCall

DEDICATION

This book is dedicated to God the Holy Spirit. It was He that led me to write this book. It was His revelations that enabled me to see what God was doing through the centuries and what God had planned for the future. Without His inspiration and favor, there would be no book. I also want to thank my wife, Lenora, who encouraged me to write.

PREFACE

I WROTE THIS BOOK BECAUSE the Holy Spirit wouldn't let me walk away from the life and legacy of Obed-Edom.

That is strange because I have never once heard a sermon on Obed-Edom. There are two accounts in this book. One account is the history of the Golden Ark of the Covenant and its ultimate disappearance, as a transition to the new covenant in the blood and body of Jesus Christ, that was foretold by prophets but not seen by the people of this book. When Jesus came, in the fulness of time, there was no ark in the Temple. In fact, there was a period of prophetic and scriptural silence of about 400 years before John the Baptist appeared to prepare the way for God's Son to introduce a new covenant. The old covenant had been broken repeatedly by the original people of the covenant. The other account is of Obed-Edom, his family, clan, and their descendants. Theirs is a story of honoring God and the things of God above all else. We see how King David was impacted by this and how the descendants of Obed-Edom were not only faithful but were used again, and again, and again, to preserve the Ark of the Covenant. For this, God blessed them and honored them through their generations. It is a lesson to us to seek first the kingdom of God and His righteousness.

ACKNOWLEDGMENTS

THE KING JAMES VERSION of the Holy Bible served as the sourcebook for this fictional account. Although fictional, this book is based on what is recorded in the Bible. Where dialogue is taken from the Bible, it was paraphrased by the author into modern colloquial English. Other dialogue comes from the artistic license of the author.

Scripture quotations are from The Authorized (King James) Version. Rights in the Authorized Version in the United Kingdom are vested in the Crown and are reproduced by permission of the Crown's patentee, Cambridge University Press.

ENDORSEMENTS

One of my favorite scriptural accounts is the passage in Luke 24:13-27, where the risen Lord Jesus expounded to two disciples on the road to Emmaus the scriptures concerning Himself from the books of Moses and the prophets. There is a climactic chapter of *He Chose the Glory* where that approach, from the Pentateuch and prophets, up to that point in time, are used to enlighten concerning the transition leading from the Golden Ark of the Covenant, and its place in worship, to the Messiah, Jesus Christ. This entire unique book will grip you with the story of how one man's honor for God and the holy things impacted how worship was done in King David's Tent and gave birth to a family legacy that has its own special place in the story of our faith.

Mark Batterson
New York Times best-selling author of *The Circle Maker*
Lead Pastor of National Community Church

Louis is a man of deep conviction, diligent study, and insightful wisdom. I can attest that his wisdom goes beyond the pen; he lives it out in word and deed, and I am a better man for crossing paths with him regularly.

Louis has uncovered one of the hidden gems of scripture in the Old Testament. This story is one that has to be told! And its wisdom needs to be unearthed. It takes a deep, thoughtful mind like Louis to bring this conversation to today's culture. No matter your position of power, Louis teaches that your commitment and resolve bring about God's destined purposes! Allow this anointed voice to speak encouragement into your soul.

I pray your heart may be animated and your mind be enlightened as you take a walk through this powerful passage of scripture.

Pastor Joel Schmidgall
National Community Church,
Capitol Hill Washington, District of Columbia

If you have ever struggled to make sense of the Hebrew Bible, the role of ancient prophets, and the Ark of the Covenant and its relevance to contemporary Christianity, struggle no more. Louis does an excellent job synthesizing an otherwise disjointed historical narrative into a beautiful and engaging fictional first-person account of ancient Israel. You will gain a deeper appreciation of the Ark of the Covenant and the blessing of honoring God's Presence. Biblical characters are brought to life in ways you've never seen them. The book is a concise page-turner that will leave you craving for more. I definitely recommend this book to be on every Christian leader's bookshelf. Get and read it!

Pastor Kelvin Kings
Mulembe Arlington Temple United Methodist Church
Arlington, Virginia

While reading *He Chose the Glory*, I came to the understanding that Obed-Edom knew two things: (1) He knew that it was more than about the Ark that was made out of wood, wrapped in gold. He knew that it was more than about the cherubim and the mercy seat. He knew that it was actually about the God who instructed them to build it. (2) Obed-Edom knew that it was about something else. It was about being ready for God to bless us. In the morning, be ready for God to bless. In the evening, be ready for God.

On noonday, be ready for God to bless. The only way I know how to say this is, we need to realize that, at the most inconvenient times, God chooses to pour out His blessing. At times, when we don't expect it, God chooses to pour out His blessing. If we are seeking and are ready, think of how much we will be prepared for God pouring out His blessing.

TABLE OF CONTENTS

You will love reading *He Chose the Glory*. I also found myself cross-referencing scriptures throughout this amazing book to have more of an in-depth understanding of how the author portrayed God's purpose and blessings over us and our lineage. Mr. McCall is truly an anointed man of God.

Pastor Andre Woods
One Love Ministries Washington,
District of Columbia

I was deeply honored to write this endorsement for the book *He Chose the Glory*. The book showed what it means to be in a covenant relationship with God. It was an easy read but full of knowledge. Always choose the Glory.

Elder Linda S. Greene,
Pastor New Beginning Church Lipscomb,
Alabama

CHAPTER 1

Jerusalem Under Siege

For then the king of Babylon's army besieged Jerusalem: and Jeremiah the prophet was shut up in the court of the prison, which was in the king of Judah's house.

Jeremiah 32:2

The Prophet Cries Out

I am Hadar. I am a Levite descended from the clan of Obed-Edom. Our clan was also descended from Merari, one of the three sons of Aaron, the first high priest. It was the Levites that had the honor of transporting, by portering on their shoulders, the Ark of the Covenant from the time of Moses. From my post at the entrance to the Temple, as one of the Temple guards, I could see him. Day after day, the prophet Jeremiah would come and walk along the parapet of the city wall. As he did so, his brown striped robes and mantle billowed and flapped in the wind coming off the valley. His hair likewise seemed to be alive and moving every which way. Jeremiah would proclaim his message loudly, as he was doing this day, for all who had been peering over the ramparts, soldiers and city folk, and to those gathering on the street below to hear.

He said our God was punishing us for our disobedience in that we had been sacrificing to idol gods, principally to Baal and Molech, and had not kept His commandment to give this promised land its regular sabbaths. So, God had allowed the Chaldeans of Babylonia, under Emperor Nebuchadnezzar, to come and lay siege to Jerusalem. Jeremiah preached that we should surrender to the Chaldeans and go willingly into captivity in Babylon so that the land would have the sabbath rests that had been denied by our disobedience, and the people would be chastened for a number of years for the idolatry they had permitted. That idolatry went so far as to offer their own infant children to Molech as human sacrifices, burned alive in the heated brass arms of that idol in the valley just outside the walls of Jerusalem. However, there was the promise that the people would eventually return, regain their lands, and serve God. For those that would not heed his words, which he said were from God, Jeremiah foretold a grim fate.

Life Under Siege

In the meantime, out of bow shot from our archers on the wall, the invading army of Chaldeans covered the hillsides surrounding Jerusalem. We could see the siege ramps the Chaldeans had built to storm the city walls once they were ready for their attack. It was a sobering sight.

Jerusalem itself was overcrowded. As the army of the empire of Babylon had advanced from the north, many people in the lesser towns had fled to the fortified cities of Lachish, Azekah, and Jerusalem in Judah for what they thought would be a secure refuge; even though a good number of the poorer folk were forced to live in the streets and squares. Besides, the Temple was here in Jerusalem. Daily, the Temple was filled with crowds praying and calling out to God for deliverance.

We had water in cisterns, wells, pools, and from subterranean streams, but the stores of food had to be rationed since it wasn't possible to venture safely beyond the city walls to the fields. Even though the Levites had their traditional garden plots near the city walls, it was extremely hazardous to try and slip out, even under cover of darkness, to reap some of the things growing there. Pity the poor bird overflying the city that thought to alight somewhere. Bird catchers with nets would try and snag them for a modest meal.

Those who had hoarded food thought themselves rich from the exorbitant prices they charged for a measure of their grain. We were under famine conditions. Everyone's garments were loose upon them by reason of losing weight due to the famine. In addition, with houses full of extra guests who had fled to Jerusalem and the streets full of the homeless, sickness and pestilence had started to spread.

An Unwelcome Message

As the siege wore on, some of the people murmured about going out to the Chaldeans to surrender and give themselves up to become servants of the Emperor of Babylon. So, to stop the slide toward surrender, King Zedekiah had Jeremiah brought into his palace for questioning and to receive a warning. King Zedekiah himself interrogated Jeremiah. King Zedekiah demanded of Jeremiah: "Why have you been going about Jerusalem, a city under siege, saying the Lord told you He was going to give Jerusalem to the pagan Babylonian Emperor and that even I, the king, will not escape, but be taken captive to Babylon? Moreover, you have weakened the morale of the troops defending us by saying even if they fight, their resistance will be futile, and this great city will fall."

Jeremiah spoke in reply by prophecy. He spoke the Lord's words saying, "The Emperor of Babylon will indeed take Jerusalem and set it to the torch to burn it down. Also, you, my king, will not escape but be carried off to Babylon as a captive."

Jeremiah went on to explain that the houses of the city would be burned because the people had angered the Lord by burning incense and pouring out oblations to pagan gods from their rooftops. The people had also put images of idols in the Temple and erected places of worship to the pagan gods Baal and Molech in the valley outside the city. There they made human sacrifices of their own infants to Molech.

Jeremiah didn't prophesy judgment and death only. He also spoke words of hope from the Lord. He said the day would come when God would restore His people to the land and give them peace. Jeremiah also prophesied that God would keep His promises to Judah and Israel and to David. He spoke of a future day in which a Messiah out of the royal line of David would rule, and the people would have a glorious future.

Descent into Rebellion that Brought Judgment

For my part, I wept frequently and wondered how we had come to the situation in which we had found ourselves. It was depressing to recall that, under King David and his son, King Solomon, the kingdom was united and had expanded up to the Euphrates River. Our enemies had been defeated. Kings came from far and near bearing gifts, paying tribute, and seeking audiences with David and Solomon. Every child knew the story of the Queen of Sheba, for example. She came with a great retinue and gifts to see for herself what she had heard of King Solomon and listen to his wisdom.

The kingdom divided under Solomon's heir, Rehoboam, with ten northern tribes going their own way, as the Kingdom of Israel, and Judah, together with little Benjamin, being left to the house of David. Both kingdoms slid into or tolerated idolatry. A few good kings did try to lead in righteousness, but both kingdoms angered God. So instead of ruling the surrounding nations, both the Kingdom of Judah and the Kingdom of Israel, besides fighting civil wars with each other, were plagued by the resurgence of their surrounding enemies, Syria, Philistia, and Edom, among others. In addition, both Judah and Israel began to be fought over and subjugated, in turn, by the empires of Egypt, from the south, and from the north by the Empires of Assyria and then Babylon.

Israel received the most severe judgment first. The people of Israel gave up coming to the Temple in Jerusalem because it was in Judah, and their king gave them an idolatrous alternative in Israel, lest they seek reconciliation with Judah. They erected their own places of worship and set up the Egyptian calf idol Aphis. They became almost indistinguishable from the pagans to their north in the things they did. Finally, almost a century and a half ago, the Assyrians swept through Israel. Those they did not kill they carried away captive and replaced them with peoples from other parts of their empire. A few inhabitants of Israel remained intermarried with these pagan people that had been resettled in their lands.

After having disposed of Israel, the Assyrian Emperor, Sennacherib, decided to return and take the kingdom of Judah in like manner. At the time, King Hezekiah tried to placate Emperor Sennacherib by offering to pay a heavy tribute of silver and gold. To do so, Hezekiah had to strip gold from the Temple. The Assyrians weren't satisfied for long and returned with a huge army and mouthing threats. This time King Hezekiah presented the matter to the prophet Isaiah and prayed for God to deliver Jerusalem and the Kingdom of Judah from these Assyrians who bragged how no other people or their gods had been able to stand against them. King Hezekiah prayed to the Lord, spreading a letter from the Assyrians before the Lord in the Temple. Hezekiah prayed to the Lord, saying that Sennacherib was defying God.

God Fights for a Nation

God answered the prayer of Hezekiah with a response delivered by the prophet Isaiah. God assured King Hezekiah that the Emperor of Assyria would not enter Jerusalem or even put siege ramps up against the city walls. In fact, God announced that He would Himself defend Jerusalem and save it for His own sake and in memory of King David. Overnight, an angel of the Lord killed 185,000 Assyrians.

That forced Emperor Sennacherib to leave the dead bodies of his army behind and return to his capital of Nineveh in Assyria. There, two of his own sons turned on him and assassinated him with their swords. Perhaps, it was in recalling this history that some hoped another angel would come and deliver us from the Chaldeans.

Pawn in a Great Power Game

After the withdrawal of the Assyrians from the Kingdom of Judah, and the gradual decline, over the years, of the Assyrian Empire, the Chaldeans of Babylonia and their allies strengthened and determined to take on Assyria directly. In order to honor a secret treaty between Egypt and Assyria and maintain the balance of power to keep Babylon from becoming a threat to Egypt, Pharaoh Necho II of Egypt led his army northward through Judah to support his Assyrian allies. However, without consulting God, King Josiah of Judah went out against Pharaoh Necho II in the Valley of Meggido. Pharaoh Necho II pleaded with King Josiah that he had no designs on Judah and did not want to fight him so that he could go fight against the Chaldeans in support of Assyria. However, King Josiah would not listen. Josiah engaged the Egyptians and was mortally wounded in battle.

Thus, our current downfall began to play out. Josiah was a good king, but he made a big mistake that cost him his life and the independence of the Kingdom of Judah. Josiah left three sons. In rapid order, each of them, in turn, and the son of one of the three brothers, ruled Judah until Zedekiah, our present king.

First, Pharaoh Necho II went on northward from Meggido to Carchemish, in Syria, and to the Euphrates River to help the Assyrians, whose major city, Ninevah, had already been overthrown by the rebellious Chaldeans and their allies. The Chaldeans and their allies were too strong. Pharaoh Necho II then withdrew to Carchemish, where he was defeated in a battle that confirmed the ascendency of Babylon.

As Pharaoh Necho II returned to Egypt, he took captive King Josiah's son Jehoahaz, who had succeeded King Josiah, and had just begun to reign and made Judah pay tribute as a vassal kingdom. Pharaoh Necho II set up Jehoahaz's older brother Eliakim, whom he renamed Jehoiakim, on the throne of Judah while taking Jehoahaz captive to Egypt.

After a few years, the king of Babylon, as Babylon continued to rise in power, sent his son Nebuchadnezzar, the crown prince, to lay siege on Egypt. Nebuchadnezzar was ultimately able to get Egypt to pay tribute to Babylon.

Jehoiakim reigned eleven years and was succeeded by his eighteen-year-old son Jehoiachin, who was also known as Jeconiah and Coniah. During the reign of Jehoiakim,

Nebuchadnezzar, who had become Emperor over the Babylonian empire, invaded Judah and made Judah and King Jehoiakim, his vassal, plucking them out of the control of Egypt. After three years, King Jehoiakim rebelled against Babylon. His son succeeded him in a brief rule as the Chaldeans invaded Judah again and increased its rule of the land. Egypt did not dare intervene on behalf of Judah at that time. The young King Jehoiachin was taken captive to Babylon along with his royal court, the military officers, and 10,000 other captives. Nebuchadnezzar then installed as king of Judah, Zedekiah, Jehoiachin's uncle, who was also the third and last son of King Josiah.

King Zedekiah, my king, whose name was Mattaniah before Nebuchadnezzar changed it, presided over a weakened kingdom. The best people had been taken captive to Babylon. After nine years of his reign, King Zedekiah, who was a vassal of Babylon, entered into a pact with Egypt to throw off the control of Babylon and declared an open revolt. This provoked the Chaldeans to invade Judah again, bringing us to the situation in which we have now found ourselves.

When the Chaldeans, who had laid siege to Jerusalem, learned that the Egyptian army was on the move from the south, they withdrew from Judah, temporarily, to confront the Egyptians. The Egyptians were still a great power themselves and preferred that Judah be a buffer between Egypt and the Babylonian empire. However, when the

Chaldeans arrayed before the Egyptian army for battle, the Egyptians retreated back to Egypt, and the Chaldeans eventually returned to continue the siege of Jerusalem and the other fortified cities of Judah.

During the hiatus, when the Chaldeans left off the siege of Jerusalem to deal with the Egyptian threat, the people were able to go out once again to gather food and fodder.

Everyone knew the Chaldeans would eventually return since they at least had to pass that way to return to Babylon once they finished their matter with the Egyptians. In an attempt to do a righteous thing and to get the people to be united in the struggle against the Chaldeans, King Zedekiah decreed that every slave owner in Jerusalem should emancipate their Hebrew slaves. All of the officials and persons of wealth gathered at the Temple, agreed to this compact and released their Hebrew slaves. However, they later reneged on the agreement and re-enslaved the people.

At that time, Jeremiah stood up and spoke words given to him from the Lord by prophecy. He reminded the people that it was God's pact that Hebrews that had sold themselves into bondage to another of their countrymen had to be released every seventh year. Their ancestors had not kept this covenant, and now they, by forcing people who had been freed to submit to slavery again, had further angered the Lord. So, the prophecy Jeremiah spoke of was harsh. The Lord, through Jeremiah, said He would bring the Chaldeans back to Jerusalem. The Chaldeans would take Jerusalem and the other cities and towns of Judah, carrying out a horrible massacre and burning Jerusalem and the other towns of Judah so utterly that the land would not be habitable.

Words of Warning

Because Jeremiah's freedom was restricted, such that he was not allowed to go to the Temple, he had Baruch come to him with a blank scroll. Sitting in his home, Jeremiah dictated to Baruch the words the Lord had given him prophetically and told Baruch to go to the Temple in his place and read the scroll so that the people who had come in from the surrounding towns could hear those words. It was hoped that the people would repent, turn from wickedness, and petition the Lord for mercy. After completing the scroll, Baruch did as he was instructed and went to the Temple where he publicly read the contents of the scroll. Word of this got back to officials in the royal palace, and they sent for Baruch to read the words of the scroll to them.

After giving Baruch an audience and hearing the words of the scroll, which Baruch dramatically spoke as though Jeremiah himself was present and speaking, the palace officials were struck with fear and determined to report the contents of the scroll to King Zedekiah. After learning that Baruch got the words of the scroll from Jeremiah, the officials warned Baruch to hide, together with Jeremiah, while they took the matter to the king. Upon hearing their report, the king sent for the scroll and had it read to him. After each section was read, the king would cut it out with a small knife and tossed each scrap into a firepot he had been warming himself with until the entire scroll was burned piece by piece. Then the king called for the arrest of Baruch and Jeremiah, but they could not be found.

During the time the Chaldeans were busy dealing with the Egyptians, Jeremiah was able to get away to the land of the tribe of Benjamin, but it didn't go well with him there. The leaders in Benjamin accused Jeremiah of being a collaborator with the Chaldeans and a traitor. Accordingly, they physically abused Jeremiah and put him in a dungeon. There Jeremiah got no food, and he shivered from the cold and dampness of that dungeon.

CHAPTER 2

Hard Time in a Dungeon

Before I formed thee in the belly I knew thee; and before thou camest forth out of the womb I sanctified thee, and I ordained thee a prophet unto the nations. Then said I, Ah Lord GOD! Behold, I cannot speak: for I am a child. But the LORD said unto me, Say not, I am a child: for thou shalt go to all that I shall send thee, and whatsoever I command thee thou shalt speak. Be not afraid of their faces: for I am with thee to deliver thee, saith the LORD.

Jeremiah 1:5-8

No Way to Treat a Prophet

King Zedekiah ordered Jeremiah to be brought to him. Jeremiah begged not to be sent back to the dungeon in Benjamin for fear he would die there. The king granted Jeremiah's request and had him held in the court of the prison in the palace with a daily ration of bread, as long as bread was to be had. In the meantime, King Zedekiah sought a comforting word from God, but Jeremiah could only repeat what he had told the king before.

Finally, a group of nobles went to King Zedekiah and demanded that Jeremiah be thrown into the king's palace dungeon. They argued that the prophet Jeremiah was damaging the morale of the troops defending the city. King Zedekiah, being in a weakened position, gave in to the vengeful nobles in order to placate them.

Jeremiah was put in the king's dungeon located under the royal treasury. The king regretted this action but was fearful of displeasing the nobles. Besides, his military leaders had also been pleading with him to get Jeremiah to be quiet for concern people would try to break out of the city and create a breach that would allow the Chaldeans to rush in and take the city.

No sooner had Jeremiah been thrown into the lower dungeon than he began to struggle to stand upright. The ground underneath him was not solid. There in the darkness and stench, Jeremiah realized he was slowly sinking in the cold muck. He ceased his struggles to slow being swallowed by the muck. Jeremiah began to despair of ever seeing the sun again or even having another meal before meeting his end in that wretched dungeon.

A Foreigner from Africa Saves Jeremiah

Ebed-Melech, a eunuch in the king's court entrusted with securing the king's harem, was a tall, handsome, black-skinned Ethiopian. The Hebrew name given to him means servant of the king. Ebed-Melech, by reason of his position as keeper of the royal harem, had access to the king. While King Zedekiah was sitting in a place of judgment adjudicating the issues of the people brought before him, Ebed-Melech approached closely and, in confidence, pleaded to the king on behalf of Jeremiah so that Jeremiah would not die in the dungeon. It was left to this foreigner to call out the evil deeds of the nobility and force the king to judge himself. Ebed-Melech's arguments won the day, and the king finally began to show some backbone. King Zedekiah then told Ebed-Melech to round up thirty men and get Jeremiah out of the dungeon.

Ebed-Melech sought out trustworthy men because of the plotting against Jeremiah and the opposition of the nobles. He got some of the keepers of the king's treasury and members of the Obed-Edom clan that guarded the treasury of the Temple since the Temple treasury guards were of the same guild as the royal treasury guards. These Temple guards, which included me, joked that Ebed was our cousin because of the similarities of our names since the meaning of the names Obed and Ebed, each referred to servants.

By now, the prophet Jeremiah had sunk up to his chest in the mire of the dungeon. It would be no easy task to extract him without tearing him apart as the suction forces of the mire would pull to keep the prophet bound until he would die there. However, Ebed-Melech was very wise. He took worn-out clothes and old rags and ordered us to braid them into a soft fat rope. We let these down into the dungeon to Jeremiah. Ebed-Melech then instructed Jeremiah to slip the rope of rags under his arms and hold on. Slowly but steadily, we drew the prophet up out of the power of the mire of the dungeon and then raised him fully out of that foul place and removed him to the court of the guards.

Honoring and Preserving the Ark

After being removed to a safe place within the palace complex, Jeremiah, still breathing heavily from the ordeal and yet covered in slimy mire, beckoned Ebed-Melech and the Obed-Edom clan members of the Temple guards to gather around him while the royal treasury guards were thanked, blessed, and dismissed. We had a special connection with Jeremiah because he, too, was a Levite and also the son of a priest. Jeremiah told us that the Chaldeans would soon take the city, as God had shown him and as he had faithfully prophesied. He stressed to us that it was important that the Ark of the Covenant with its contents not fall into the hands of the Chaldeans.

The last time Nebuchadnezzar came down to Judah, he took King Jehoiakim captive and a host of captives together with King Jehoiakim. Nebuchadnezzar also stripped silver and gold from the Temple, including the holy vessels. He did not get the Ark and a few other sacred implements of gold, including the Golden Lampstand, and the Golden Table of the Presence, because those things had been hidden away safely by us of the clan of Obed-Edom. They were again placed back in the Temple once Nebuchadnezzar and his army of Chaldeans had withdrawn to Babylon.

Jeremiah told us how, during the reign of King Josiah, God's Word came to him concerning Israel, which had been dispersed into captivity by the Assyrians, although Judah had become as wayward as Israel. The Lord then had Jeremiah prophesy concerning Israel that the day would come when He would bring the people of Israel back into the land with the people of Judah where they would multiply. On that day, he prophesied: "Men would stop talking about the Ark of the Covenant. They won't even remember it. It won't even pass across their minds. The Ark won't even be missed, nor will another be made, but, at that time, they will call Jerusalem God's throne. Peoples from all of the nations of the earth will come to Jerusalem to honor the Lord's Name."

Although Jeremiah couldn't see it then, he now realized that the Ark of the Covenant must be taken from Jerusalem and hidden away for the prophecy to come to pass. Jeremiah then directed us to undertake the mission of, once again, removing the Ark to a safe place so that it would not fall into the hands of the godless Chaldean invaders from Babylon.

Jeremiah also informed us how, in about the fifth through the eight years of King Zedekiah's reign, God revealed to the prophet Ezekiel, who was with the captives in Babylon, that the Shekinah glory of God had gradually lifted up and been removed from the Ark of the Covenant, out of the Temple, out of the city, and to the mountains, before being completely withdrawn. This was because of the sin of the people in Judah that had persisted in worshiping idols so that God's Shekinah Glory would no longer abide above the Mercy Seat of the Ark or in the Temple or with His people. God had shown Ezekiel that the army of Babylon would return to Jerusalem, set up a siege ramp, battering rams, and siege machines to take Jerusalem and slaughter most of the people, except for those whose spirits were distressed by the idolatry that the people had given themselves over to serving. The Lord also showed Ezekiel that King Zedekiah would try to escape only to be chased down and have his eyes put out before being taken captive to Babylon. Ezekiel had revealed this to the captives, and word also reached Jeremiah. However, as the Lord had also revealed to Jeremiah, Ezekiel prophesied there would be a future time when God would bring the people back and give them hearts to serve Him. That whole message from God was grim news. We knew we had to move quickly to do what Jeremiah was charging us to do. In addition, we had to act without delay to save ourselves and our families.

It had been many generations since the Ark was initially moved into King Solomon's Temple. As Levites of the branch of Merari, one of Aaron the high priest's three sons, we were of those who could porter the Ark on our shoulders, as had been established by Moses. So, we, as the prophet's rescuers, and others of our clan who guarded the Temple and worshipped with other musicians on the Temple grounds, made plans to flee the city with the Ark and our families. We took Ebed-Melech with us. Besides, he knew of hidden passageways under the city of David in the event the king's household had to flee. Also, since he orchestrated the deliverance of the prophet, who chose to stay behind, it was only right that he should come with us and be spared the calamity about to fall on Jerusalem. As a eunuch in charge of the king's harem, he had no family to accompany him. I told him he would always be welcome among my family and our clan.

CHAPTER 3

Flight to Safety

> But thou shalt appoint the Levites over the tabernacle of testimony, and over all the vessels thereof, and over all things that belong to it: they shall bear the tabernacle, and all the vessels thereof; and they shall minister unto it, and shall encamp round about the tabernacle.
>
> Numbers 1:50

I GATHERED OUR CLAN TOGETHER and laid out our plan. During a late-night watch, we would take the Ark of the Covenant from the Temple and, together with our families, including a few Levite priests that had married into our family and who were trusted, flee the city under cover of darkness. There was no time to spare. The prophet Jeremiah was emphatic about the need to preserve the Ark from the Chaldeans who were soon to take Jerusalem.

Of course, I had the women present at our meeting. I charged all to consecrate themselves for the task before us and refrain from marital relations until we could complete our mission. To the women would fall the task of keeping the young ones quiet. Any cooking utensils would have to be wrapped in a cloth to avoid clanging and giving away our movement. Mariam, my widowed mother, spoke up.

That was a bold thing for her to do since this was men's business, and women didn't speak unless they were called upon. Letting her shawl drop to her shoulders and tossing back her long gray hair, as if to remind others of the respect due to the hoary gray head, she said:

> "Hadar, my son, I must, with your permission, say a word on behalf of the women. We will do our part, and we realize the men have their part, especially in the holy duty of portering the Ark of the Covenant and fighting with weapons, if necessary. However, for those women with several children, including nursing infants, it is too much to ask them to make this trek in haste while keeping her children together, soothing infants, and carrying pots, plates, cups, clothes, and bedding without help. Please remind the men to be sensitive and to assist us. It won't make them any less the man and will help us all move faster and quieter together."

> "My dear mother," I said, "we truly have to do this as a community and a close clan. Your words

have practical wisdom. I will see to it that the young women are not over-burdened." Then I added, "Men, are we agreed?" as one, the stout men and the very young men replied, "Yes, Hadar, we are agreed!"

Inside the Temple, we had a group of our clan take down the curtain that divided the Holy Place from the Most Holy Place where the Ark of the Covenant was kept. They kept their backs to the Ark and walked backward to the Ark to lay the curtain over it, being careful not to touch the actual Ark with their hands. In the days of Moses, the Levites that bare the Ark on their shoulders also covered it with the curtain that divided the Holy Place from the Most Holy Place in the tabernacle of Moses when the Ark had to be moved in alignment with the movement of the manifestation of God's Glory. Of course, this made the golden Ark that much heavier because the curtain itself was thick, sturdy, and heavy. We also decided that we would take the Golden Lampstand and the Golden Table of the Presence, which held the showbread, and the altar of incense, rather than let them fall into the hands of the Chaldeans. In taking the Table of the Presence, we also took the loaves of bread that were on it. I recalled that David took the bread of the Presence when he fled from King Saul. Why not us? Besides, we would need it.

Hezekiah's Tunnel and a Canaanite Water Shaft

Under the city of David were King Hezekiah's tunnel and other tunnels to cisterns. Hezekiah's tunnel dug during the invasion of the Assyrians, brought the Gihon Spring under the walls of the city of David, and sent the waters to the Pool of Siloam where the waters could be safely drawn without being exposed to an enemy. Ebed-Melech led the way for us with the bearers of the Ark close behind. While under the city, we used torches and oil lamps to light the dark tunnel passageways. In some places, it was wet and slippery. Men, women, and children stumbled and fell into shallow pools of water along the way.

Finally, Ebed-Melech led us to one of the narrow openings that the ancient Canaanites of Jebus, the Jebusite fortified city, had dug to serve as water shafts. These Canaanite tunnels led outside to the base of the city walls in the Kidron Valley. It was by the grace of God that Ebed-Melech led us to an old Canaanite tunnel with a wide enough passageway to get the Ark through without it being damaged. When we neared the exit, Ebed-Melech beckoned for guards to come forward to cut away the brush that had overgrown the opening. Once that was accomplished, we filed out, without the torches and lamps, hunched over or crawling, as the porters of the Ark had to do, to make it through the opening.

Dash for Life

There was a crescent moon that night that provided our only light. We moved with purpose and stealth. We did not want our own archers on the wall to strike us with their arrows. We also did not want to draw the attention of the Chaldeans. Fortunately, the Chaldeans did not have forces close to the city walls. They were also supremely confident that our army would not risk all in an attack against them under cover of darkness. Nevertheless, we hastily made our way down into the Kidron Valley and then up a hillside where we did not see campfires of the enemy Chaldeans. We had to frequently switch out the bearers of the Ark while on the march because its combined weight with the covering curtain wearied those with that holy burden.

The smallest children had been given a drink laced with an herb that my mother Mariam concocted that put them to sleep. Their mothers carried them in their arms. When a young child would stir to awaken, its mother would quickly put it to suck on her breast to avoid any cry. Here in the field, our armed guards went ahead to ensure we did not stumble upon a troop of Chaldeans. In the event that should happen, they knew their task was to slit the throats of the enemy as they slumbered or otherwise dispatch them to avoid a call to arms. We men had played in these hills as children and relied on our knowledge to get us beyond the hills to a place where we knew there were caves. These were places the shepherds used to hold some of their sheep overnight before bringing their flock to the city for sacrifice or to be sold to the butchers to prepare for their patrons.

As the dawn approached, our pace quickened. We could not allow ourselves to be caught out in the open with the Ark and the women and children. In our haste, we stopped using hand signals and began to urgently plead under our breath for everyone to move with all speed while maintaining quietness toward the place where our forward guards were leading us. Time and again, a small child would stumble over roots or a stone and fall hard and awkwardly only to be swiftly swept up and comforted by a father or uncle so that they would not cry and expose us to the enemy. At last, we reached a series of shepherd's caves. One cave was large enough to take our whole company. We threw ourselves down once inside. We were exhausted, heaving and breathing heavily, sweat pouring down from the exertion of our forced march with the Ark, the Golden Lampstand, Golden Table of the Presence, the Altar of Incense, and women and children. There would be no fires for light, warmth, or cooking and no one was to venture outside again without my command or instruction. I instructed some of the guards to cut brush to place at the opening of our cave to obscure the entrance and not draw attention to our presence there. The cave was dark. As we moved about, we stumbled over each other and excused ourselves to keep the peace. Then we witnessed an amazing miracle as the Ark of the Covenant, still covered by the curtains from the Temple, began to glow. This provided light and was a witness to us all that the Spirit of the Lord was with us in this undertaking.

CHAPTER 4

Enemy on the Move

> Then came the Word of the LORD unto the prophet Jeremiah, saying, Thus saith the LORD, the God of Israel, Thus shall ye say to the king of Judah, that sent you unto Me to enquire of Me; Behold, Pharaoh's army, which is come forth to help you, shall return to Egypt into their own land. And the Chaldeans shall come again, and fight against this city, and take it, and burn it with fire.
>
> Jeremiah 37:6-8

Preparing for the Fatal Attack

As the morning broke, we could hear the Chaldeans begin to stir. The end was not far off for Jerusalem. We could see the city from our refuge in the cave. The Chaldeans were not yet ready to end the siege and make a direct attack, but they began to move their siege machines into place, with the help of their horses, and hastily completed the construction of ramps to get their wall breaching machines and battering rams on paths to launch a multi-pronged assault on Jerusalem.

Thank God we were not in the line of attack. We huddled in the cave and quietly prayed toward the Temple, asking for God's mercy and confessing our sins as a people and individually. We ate some of the precious rations of bread we managed to bring with us, which included some loaves of the Presence bread we plucked from the Temple in the process of removing the Ark, the Golden Table of the Presence, and the Golden Lampstand, and the Altar for burning incense, but otherwise, we laid low.

We could hear the mourning coming up from the city. The people of Jerusalem knew the end was near. We wondered, would God send an angel as He did in a past time to slay a vast army of Assyrians when Hezekiah was king of Judah? Would the people heed the words of prophet Jeremiah and surrender to the Chaldean army? No one knew what the next move was to be.

The Chaldeans moved like an army of ants with a single purpose, so it seemed, as a few of the men and I dared to peek through the brush at the mouth of our cave. Our hearts went out to our countrymen in Jerusalem. We recalled how the prophet Jeremiah had pleaded for the people to go out to the Chaldeans and surrender. Was it too late for that? Was it too late for the people to confess their sins to God and beg for mercy and a miraculous intervention? More importantly, how long could we hide out safely in the cave?

We dared not make a move in eyesight in broad daylight, even with the Chaldeans having their attention fixed on Jerusalem. Fortunately, back in the rear part of the cave was a trickle of water. Although we had brought some water with us, we made sure none of that precious trickle was wasted, whether captured in a goatskin or allowed to fall directly into the mouth of a thirsty child or adult.

We were amazed at the steady progress being made by the determined Chaldeans in preparation for their final assault. This time, they would not be deterred from their attack by news of the Egyptians coming to our aid. God had once used Gideon's small force of 300 brave troops to rout a far superior force. Although the sins of our people were many, would God undertake to save our nation again despite the overwhelming odds before us?

Recalling that we had the Ark of the Covenant with us, we gathered around the still glowing Ark and prayed. Never before had we prayed with such intensity. Family units huddled together to comfort one another as we all prayed, yet being mindful not to cause our voices to be heard outside the cave.

As it began to grow dark again, the Chaldeans began an attack of terror that preceded the all-out attack surely to follow the next day. Some of their machines of war launched fire-tipped arrows over the walls of the city, setting some of the rooftops on fire. Likewise, other machines of war heaved large rocks over the walls causing havoc as those rocks smashed into homes. Other stones from those machines were aimed at the city gates to weaken them in advance of an assault on the gates by battering rams. Although we were safe from attack in the cave, our hearts went out to our friends and neighbors we knew were being terrorized through the night. We cried and trembled as we heard the cries rising up from within Jerusalem.

God Had Been Warning, But We Did Not Heed

It was Ebed-Melech who approached me and caused us to put these events in perspective. "My friend Hadar," he said, "don't you know that a century before Babylon became the powerful empire that it had become when the Assyrians were the empire to the north that ruled with a strong hand, that the Lord spoke to King Hezekiah by the prophet Isaiah concerning this very time? The king of Babylon at that time, Merodachbaladan, had sent emissaries to King Hezekiah with a letter and a gift because the king of Babylon had heard that King Hezekiah had been sick but recovered. King Hezekiah showed those emissaries all his treasures. Afterward, when the prophet Isaiah confronted King Hezekiah, the king confessed that he had shown the emissaries of the King of Babylon every precious thing that he had. Isaiah then spoke the Word of the Lord to King Hezekiah, saying, 'The days are coming when everything in your house and all that your ancestors have stored up will be carried away to Babylon: nothing will be left.'"

"Moreover, Hadar, my friend, the prophet Isaiah said to King Hezekiah by the Lord: 'The Babylonians will take away your royal descendants, and they will be castrated and made eunuchs serve in the palace of the King of Babylon.' Hadar, isn't the prophecy of Isaiah, from many years ago, what we are witnessing right now? Eleven years ago, the Babylonians came and took King Jehoiachin and many nobles captive and raided the royal treasury, and also took what they could find in the Temple and Temple storehouse. Now they have returned, in fulfillment of Isaiah's prophecy, to take all that remains."

CHAPTER 5

Recalling the History of the Ark

And thou shalt put the mercy seat above upon the Ark; and in the Ark thou shalt put the testimony that I shall give the. And there I will meet with thee, and I will commune with thee from above the mercy seat, from between the two cherubim which are upon the Ark of the testimony, of all things which I will give thee in commandment unto the children of Israel.

Exodus 25:21-22

The Story of the Ark and of Obed-Edom

I, Hadar, thought it would be best to do something to take our minds off of the clamor that was going on in and around Jerusalem. So I had our company gather around in the soft golden light being given off by the Ark to hear me.

We were the clan of Obed-Edom of the tribe of Levi. Our history was tied up with that of our ancestor Obed-Edom and the decisive choice he made concerning the Ark of the Covenant.

I said, "Listen to me well. We sit here in this cave with the very Ark of the Covenant. I believe it is good for us to recall the history of the Ark." So I began to review the history of the precious Ark from its beginning:

"You people of the clan of Obed-Edom, and our companion Ebed-Melech, it was in the desert of Sinai, after God had brought Israel up out of the bondage of Egypt, with awesome miracles, after 400 years there, that He gave Moses the plans for the Ark of the Covenant. The Ark is a chest of acacia wood covered within and without with hammered pure gold. A lid of solid pure gold, known as the mercy seat, with two facing cherubim of pure gold, rests on the chest. This lid, with the two cherubim on top, was called the 'mercy seat' because the stone tablets of the law were inside the chest. Without God coming in His mercy, no one could avoid judgment and death. Four rings of pure gold were made for the corners. Through those rings were put two poles of acacia wood for carrying the Ark. Once fashioned and sanctified, no man was permitted to touch the Ark again, except as instructed by God. Those poles, once inserted, have never been removed, and it is those poles that we, as Levites, placed on our shoulders to remove the

Ark from the Temple to this cave where we now take shelter."

"God promised that He would speak with Moses from the space between the two cherubim. Initially, the only things in the Ark were the stone tablets God gave Moses with the ten commandments of the law. The life of the people of Israel was centered on this Ark of the Covenant. The Glory of God was there. When our ancestors wandered for forty years in the wilderness, the whole of the tribes moved when the Glory of God rose, and the Ark was moved with it. When the Glory would stop, the bearers of the Ark would stop, and the tribes would encamp around it. Space was required between the tents of the tribes and the Ark so that our ancestors could see it and the tent that served as a type of temple when the tribes were not on the march." I went on to declare:

"God's Presence was with our ancestors as a cloud of fire in the sky over the Ark at night and during the day as a shade-giving cloud in the sky over the Ark and the tents of our tribes. It was a daily wonder for all of our ancestors to see. Our enemies could see this as their caravans passed near us on their trade routes, and they would scatter from fear. They reported what they observed wherever they went so that the nations all around feared us."

When the time came for Moses to die, and God Himself buried him, God was then with Joshua as He had been with Moses. When the people of Israel came to the Jordan River, which was at flood stage, we had no boats to ferry millions of people across, nor was there a bridge to walk across. However, God once again demonstrated that His Presence was with us when the Ark went before the nation and the waters of Jordan parted and heaped up to the north as the porters of the Ark stepped into the Jordan. As they maintained their place in the center of the Jordan River, the tribes crossed over on dry ground into the promised land. Once the Ark was portered to the other bank of Jordan, the flow of the river resumed.

I described how the first city on the other side of Jordan to be conquered was Jericho. Jericho was a fortified city with walls that were wide and tall. We possessed no siege machines such as the Chaldeans have brought against Jerusalem. However, God had Joshua instruct our bands to silently march around Jericho with this Ark for six days, once each day. Then on the seventh day, our bands marched around Jericho seven times. At the completion of the seventh cycle with the Ark, trumpets blew, people shouted, and those walls came down. The inhabitants were petrified, and our ancestors annihilated them as they had been instructed to do, with the exception of Rahab and her family with her because she had hidden our spies.

I explained that the conquest of the promised land was a long campaign over many years. For years, the Ark was set up at Shiloh by Joshua. There it remained for 300 years. The priests would go there to offer sacrifices. That ended when the Ark was captured in battle by the Philistines. The system of going to Shiloh to sacrifice and worship ended with the capture of the Ark until the time of King David and his son King Solomon.

Dishonor the Ark and Die by the Ark

Saul was the first king over Israel after the times of the judges. Years before Saul became king, and before Samuel became the last judge of Israel, the chief priest at that time did not rein in his sons, who angered the Lord by their evil ways. They did not honor the Temple, the burnt offerings, the Ark, or the Presence of God. When Hophni and Phinehas, the sons of Eli, the high priest, ordered the Ark to be brought from Shiloh to the battlefield, to use as a magic charm or talisman, they thought, to ensure victory in a battle with the Philistines, they were killed, along with 30,000 other soldiers of Israel, and the Ark was captured by the Philistines and taken to their city of Ashdod. Eli fell over, broke his neck, and died at the news.

So for a time, the Ark of the Covenant was in the hands of the Philistines. First, the sons of Eli dishonored the Ark and, after their deaths and the defeat of the army of Israel, the Philistines dishonored the Ark. When the Philistines took the Ark to Ashdod, they set it up in the temple of their god Dagon, who was considered to be the father of the god Baal, to show, they supposed, the superiority of their god. Then, when they came into their temple in the morning, the image of Dagon was on its face on the ground before the Ark. So they put the image of Dagon back on its feet only to return the following morning to find that the image of Dagon had not only fallen again, but its head and hands were also severed.

God didn't just deal with the god of Philistia, but He struck the people of Ashdod with tumors and boils from a plague that caused the death of many. The leaders of Philistia decided to move the Ark from Ashdod to Gath. However, after the Ark was moved to Gath, God struck that city too with tumors, boils, and death among both young and old. So the Philistines moved the Ark of the Covenant from Gath to Ekron. The people of that city were in a panic, saying, "They have brought the Ark of Israel's God here to kill us and our people." They begged their leaders to send the Ark away for fear they would all die. They wailed that they did not want to end up like the Egyptians whom God judged with plagues and death on account of the people of Israel.

After seven months, the leaders of Philistia decided to send the Ark back to Israel. To appease the Lord, they placed a peace offering of golden tumors and golden rats, representing the carriers of the deathly plague, in a separate chest beside the Ark. Just to be certain that the plague was not a chance circumstance, the Philistines devised a plan that would confirm whether this was of our God or just bad luck. They put the Ark on a new cart hitched to cows that had recently calved. Those cows had never been trained to pull with a yoke and would also naturally want to be with their new calves that were purposely penned up away from them. The Philistines reasoned that if the cows wandered around and returned to their calves, then it would be safe to presume that the plague and deaths were all just a coincidence and bad luck.

To the astonishment of the Philistines, the cows did not struggle against the yoke and each other, nor did they turn to go back to their calves crying for their milk. Instead, the cows went straight down the road out of the territory of Philistia to the town of Beth Shemesh, a town in Israel. The Philistine leaders followed the cart to the outskirts of Beth Shemesh, but no farther. When the Philistines saw the people of Beth Shemesh celebrate and send for Levites to remove the Ark and the chest containing gold tumors and gold rats from the cart so that the two cows could be sacrificed on the spot using the wood from the cart for fire, they returned to their cities in Philistia.

I went on to explain that the men of Beth Shemesh had initially done the right thing by having Levites among them move the Ark using the poles in the gold rings. However, in their curiosity, they then dishonored the Ark. The men of Beth Shemesh lifted the lid of the Ark and peered inside. God immediately put 50,070 of the men of the town to death for dishonoring the Ark. The surviving people then sent word to the people of the nearby town of Kiriath Jearim, asking them to take possession of the Ark, but without telling them how they had been judged with death. The men of Kiriath Jearim came and took the Ark to their town and placed it in the home of Abinadab. There the Ark remained for twenty years. In the house of Abinadab for twenty years, the Ark of the Covenant was not honored; it was just there, hidden away.

The Last Judge

During that time, the prophet Samuel began to lead Israel as its judge. When the Philistines determined to attack Israel, Samuel instructed the people to put away their idol gods and serve the Lord only. After the people obeyed and turned to God, Samuel had them gather at Mizpeh, where he interceded to the Lord on their behalf. As Samuel interceded, the people fasted and prayed, repenting of their sins. But the Philistines, upon learning that the people of Israel had gathered at Mizpeh, determined to attack them there. However, after Samuel offered up a sacrifice to the Lord, God threw the Philistines into a panic with loud claps of thunder. The men of Israel, which had been afraid of the Philistines, then took heart and pursued the Philistines, slaughtering them along the way. Samuel let the people know that the Lord had helped them. Samuel continued to judge Israel and did not have other trouble from Philistia for the rest of his life.

When Samuel became old, the people demanded that he appoint a king to rule over them like the custom of the nations around them. This angered Samuel, who considered it a personal rejection, but God told him the people were not rejecting him but were rejecting God. God then instructed Samuel to anoint a king as the people wanted. Eventually, Samuel anointed Saul of the tribe of Benjamin as king.

After God used Saul to rally the people to defeat a provocation by the army of Ammon, Samuel reaffirmed that Saul was anointed to be king. Saul reigned for forty-two years. During that time, both the Philistines and the people of Amalek opposed Israel.

Because King Saul did not obey Samuel concerning the Amalekites, it created a breach, and the kingship was taken from Saul in God's eyes, although he continued to serve in that role. Eventually, before his death, Samuel anointed David, the youngest son of Jesse, of the tribe of Judah, as the future king. Samuel did this in fear of his life since he knew King Saul, whom he had stopped seeing in person, would want to kill him as a traitor. Besides, after the Lord had rejected Saul as king, Saul would descend into angry depression under the influence of an evil spirit.

David was brought into the court of King Saul to play music on his harp to soothe the rage that would come upon Saul. David went back and forth from serving King Saul to tend his father Jesse's sheep. In time, the Philistines gathered for war with Israel. Their armies faced off on opposing hills with a valley between them. The Philistine's had a champion warrior over nine feet tall named Goliath. This giant would daily blaspheme the Lord and dare the army of Israel to send out a man to fight him with the loser's side to serve the other.

The Battle Belongs to the Lord

While bringing provisions from his father, Jesse, to his brothers in the army and their captain, David became incensed by the challenge of Goliath. Notwithstanding the rebuke of his brothers, David ignored them and asked what the reward would be for the man who defeats Goliath. This came to the attention of King Saul, who appreciated the lad David's courage, but doubted he could take on Goliath. King Saul called David a "boy." David told King Saul, "No one need lose heart on account of this Philistine. I will go out and fight him." After David told King Saul how God had helped him protect his father's sheep by killing a lion and a bear, Saul let him represent Israel on the battlefield.

Goliath had armor, weapons, a shield, and an armourbearer to assist him. David had his shepherd's staff and a sling. Goliath despised David when he saw he was only a boy and cursed David by the gods of Philistia. David, for his part, was brimming with holy confidence and let Goliath know this wasn't about weapons, rather this battle belonged to the Lord, and when it would be over, the world would know that there is a God in Israel. David ran to the battle and declared he was taking on Goliath in the name of the Lord. To the surprise of all but David, David killed Goliath with a stone from his sling and cut off the giant's head with Goliath's own sword. The army of Israel, which had been demoralized, then flooded down into the valley and up the opposing hill to begin slaughtering the Philistine army all the way back to their principal cities of Gath and Ekron.

The army of Israel returned to Jerusalem with the young victorious David toting the head of Goliath. But when women came out from the towns along the way, they sang the praises of David, attributing to him the slaying of tens of thousands in comparison to King Saul slaying thousands. Saul became enraged with jealousy. The relationship between King Saul and David went down from there with Saul trying to kill David, when the evil spirit took control of him or trying to have David assassinated until David became hunted by Saul as a fugitive over a period of years. During that time, King Saul did nothing to honor the Ark by going to it, nor did King Saul return the Ark to Shiloh or have the Ark moved to Jerusalem and put in a place of honor.

CHAPTER 6

Obed-Edom Honored the Ark

> Them that honor Me I will honour, and they that despise Me shall be lightly esteemed.
>
> 1 Samuel 2:30

A Kingdom Divided, then United

Ultimately, after a number of years, the Philistines decisively defeated King Saul and three of his sons at the Battle of Mount Gilboa in the north. King Saul's army was scattered in defeat. That opened the door for David, who had been a fugitive from Saul, to reign as king, initially over Judah alone, which he did from Hebron. A civil war ensued between David's men and the men of King Saul's remaining heir. That war lasted some time until David became victorious and was made king over the entire nation of Judah and Israel.

As king of the combined kingdom, David turned to take the Jebusite fortress of Zion, which became known as the city of David after he subdued it and made it his home base. David's tactic was to send men up a water shaft gutter to get into the fortress. It was by one of these same water shaft tunnels that we made our own escape from the besieged city of Jerusalem to get to this cave. Having taken the Jebusite fortress, David moved from Hebron to Jerusalem and its quarter of the former Jebusite fortress that became known as the city of David. When the Philistines saw that David had become king of all Israel, they marshaled their whole army to take on David. But God counseled David and gave him favor and battlefield tactics to defeat the Philistines.

Lessons in Honoring the Ark

After these great successes, David decided to honor the Ark. It came into his mind to bring the Ark of the Covenant to Jerusalem and, specifically, to the city of David where he now lived. King David took 30,000 of his best troops with him to the house of Abinadab, where the Ark had been held for twenty years. Abinadab had done nothing to honor the Ark of the Covenant while it was with him. The Ark was essentially stored away, out of sight, and without access.

Unfortunately, King David made the same mistake as did the Philistines. He had the Ark placed on a new cart. One of Abinadab's sons walked before it, and another,

Uzzah, walked behind the Ark, so the Ark was dishonored as if it were just a piece of freight. When the oxen hitched to the cart stumbled, Uzzah reached out his hand to steady the Ark and was immediately slain by God's wrath, with his dead body laying on the ground beside the cart with the Ark.

Up until that point, King David's retinue had been singing songs and playing musical instruments to celebrate the journey of the Ark to Jerusalem. Now they were silent. King David was both angry with God and afraid at the same time. King David, at that point, was not willing to take the Ark on to the city of David with him. Instead, he had it taken aside to the house of Obed-Edom, located on a nearby hill, while he returned to the city of David emptyhanded.

Interior view of a church on the site believed to
be where the house of Obed-Edom stood.

Obed-Edom Honors the Ark, and God Honors Him

Back in the city of David, King David had time to come to terms with his well-meaning errors in handling the Ark of the Covenant that unintentionally dishonored the Ark. After three months of contemplation, word came to King David that the Lord had blessed Obed-Edom and his whole household because Obed-Edom had honored the Ark. Obed-Edom was blessed by God with the joy of His Presence. Obed-Edom's crops and vineyards flourished, and many of the married women of his clan became pregnant. Those that were already pregnant delivered, not in single births, but they were delivered of twins or triplets, all of them male heirs to their husbands. In addition, people flocked to the house of Obed-Edom, bearing gifts, food, and money to help adorn his home and to bless him, as they were allowed to enter his home to worship before the Ark, but without touching it or attempting to peer inside the Ark, as did the men of Beth Shemesh. So David went again on a mission to bring the Ark to the city of David. This time he now knew that the Ark was to be portered by the wooden poles through its golden rings. Also, not just anyone could porter the Ark. The Ark had to be portered by Levites as directed by Moses.

Exterior view of a church on the site believed to
be where the house of Obed-Edom stood.

When King David arrived at the house of Obed-Edom, Obed-Edom and his sons came out to greet the king and bowed low before him in reverence. Obed-Edom then motioned for the king to enter his home. As soon as King David stepped into the house of Obed-Edom, he saw the uncovered Ark of the Covenant in an honored place in the center of the house. On the floor, all around, were members of Obed-Edom's clan. They were prostrate and worshipped the Lord before the Ark. Both Obed-Edom and the king knelt down and worshipped. The Presence of the Lord was heavy in that place.

Obed-Edom then took a lyre from where it hung on a peg on the wall, and he both played and sang praises to the Lord. King David was pleased to remain in that atmosphere for a great while. Obed-Edom then passed the lyre on to King David, who remained skillful in playing stringed instruments in praise to God. So, they continued in that atmosphere of worship, honoring the Ark of the Covenant and the Presence of the Lord until King David went back outside. Once outside, David could survey his beloved Judah, all the way back to Jerusalem in the distance, from the hill on which Obed-Edom's house stood. Then David began to instruct those that were accompanying him.

Obed-Edom prostrated himself before King David and begged for the king to hear and regard his request. Obed-Edom asked that he and his clan, who were of the tribe of Levi, not be separated from the Ark, but be allowed to both porter and accompany it to the city of David and to have a part in matters pertaining to the Ark once it was in the city of David. For this honor, Obed-Edom, his father, Jeduthun, his five sons, and his clan were prepared to leave their lands and serve the ministry of the Ark of the Covenant. They were sixty-eight men plus Obed-Edom together with their wives and children.

Looking back to Jerusalem, in the far distance, from the hill on which it is believed the house of Obed-Edom stood.

King David, having seen how God had blessed Obed-Edom and how Obed-Edom honored the Ark of the Covenant, granted the petition of Obed-Edom. So Obed-Edom assisted the other Levites King David brought with him to porter the Ark. Obed-Edom also played the lyre in the procession when not actually portering the Ark. The whole procession headed toward the city of David making a joyful noise of praise in song and with their instruments. King David put on the ephod of a priest and danced and praised God at the head of the procession. When the procession reached Jerusalem and the city of David, King David still had the strength and joy to dance before the Lord with all his might. In the process, he danced out of his outer garments. The handmaidens of the palace swooned at seeing the handsome young warrior-king, who was also a great talent as a musician and psalmist, in abandon before the Lord. But Michal, David's wife and the daughter of Saul despised him. Therefore, David told her he would become even more of a spectacle and that those handmaidens would have him in honor while she would be put away like a widow.

CHAPTER 7

The New Order of the Ark in the City of David

> So he left there before the Ark of the Covenant of the LORD Asaph and his brethren, to minister before the Ark continually, as every day's work required: And Obededom with their brethren, threescore and eight; Obededom also the son of Jeduthun and Hosah to be porters.
>
> 1 Chronicles 16:37-38

Honoring the Ark in the New Order

King David set up a system of constant service before the Lord with the Ark of the Covenant in a tent he had set up in the city of David. The Tent of Moses, the original tent for the Ark of the Covenant, was taken to the high place in Gibeon, but Shiloh lost its former importance. King David dispatched the priest Zadok and other priests to serve before the Lord in Gibeon and offer up burnt offerings there. Obed-Edom's father, Jeduthun, was also sent to Gibeon to sound the trumpets, cymbals, and other instruments. Jeduthun also served as a gatekeeper.

Obed-Edom was assigned to assist Asaph with the music at the Tent of David in the city of David. He was also a gatekeeper. Some of his sons and clan members went with Obed-Edom's father, Jeduthun, to Gibeon. Others were gatekeepers or guards for the storehouse. By lot, Obed-Edom was a gatekeeper on the south gate, which is the Zion Gate, the same gate for entry into the city of David. Also, by lot, the guard of the storehouse fell to his sons and others of the clan. The storehouse was where the holy treasuries were held.

King David liked what he had seen and experienced in the house of Obed-Edom. So, unlike the former system used in the Tent of Moses, which was left at Gibeon, that had a curtain dividing the Most Holy Place with the Ark from the Holy Place, David's Tent was set up as an open concept so that all that entered could see the Ark and worship the Lord before it, just as was done in the house of Obed-Edom. The music and praise went up continually in this tent. Thus Obed-Edom and his clan chose to honor the Ark of the Covenant, with the blessing of basking in the Presence of God and His Glory, rather than the life they had known tending their lands. Since the service of the Ark and David's Tent was distributed by lot, it was possible for

Obed-Edom and members of his clan to periodically revisit their lands before returning to the city of David to resume their appointed duties.

The Ark of the Covenant had been in the house of Abinadab for twenty years without special honor. But in just three months in the house of Obed-Edom, where he and his clan treasured the opportunity to host the Ark, God not only blessed him but gave him and his clan favor with King David so that they had regular duties with other Levites in the ministry of the Ark. Obed-Edom could have continued a quiet and obscure existence in the countryside of Judah, but he chose the Glory of God, to help establish an atmosphere of continual worship and be near the Ark in whatever capacity was assigned to him. Because he honored the Ark when it was in his house, and his clan experienced that atmosphere with him, they too decided to follow him and the Ark to the city of David to serve there and at Gibeon.

CHAPTER 8

Honoring and Preserving the Ark Through the Years

> And it came to pass in the fifth year of King Rehoboam, that Shishak King of Egypt came up against Jerusalem: And he took away the treasures of the house of the LORD, and the treasures of the king's house; he even took away all: and he took away all the shields of gold which Solomon had made.
>
> 1 Kings 14:25-26

Narrow Escapes of the Ark

King Solomon's son Rehoboam, who reigned after him, did not follow after the Lord as did his grandfather, King David, or his father, King Solomon, did in the early years of his reign. He was also foolish. Because of this and his father King Solomon's mistakes in his later years, which included building altars to the idol gods of his foreign wives so they might continue in their pattern of ungodly worship, God allowed the ten northern tribes to be stripped from Rehoboam never to be reunited. Rehoboam's mother was from Ammon due to King Solomon marrying foreign women who were princesses for political and alliance reasons.

Rehoboam led Judah in the idolatry of his mother, building places of idol worship in high places, including images of idol gods and groves that were a part of the traditional worship of the peoples that God instructed Moses and Joshua to drive from the land. Therefore, God allowed King Shishak of Egypt to raid Jerusalem and strip the Temple of Solomon of its treasures and items from the royal treasury. Shishak did not capture the Ark of the Covenant at that time because the clan of Obed-Edom, who were Temple gatekeepers and Temple storehouse guards, had removed the Ark and hid it. Nevertheless, there was humiliation in that the riches and holy vessels of the Temple had been taken away by King Shishak.

Some generations afterward, during one of the civil wars between the Kingdoms of Judah and Israel, King Jehoash of Israel attacked Jerusalem and broke down a portion of its wall after defeating King Amaziah of Judah's forces. Jehoash, too, took all the gold and silver vessels from the Temple and everything from the royal treasury. Once again, the Temple gatekeepers and Temple storehouse guards of the clan of Obed-Edom hid away safely the Ark of the

Covenant, the Golden Lampstand, and the Golden Table of the Presence until King Jehoash returned to Samaria.

Now, in our own time, we have seen Nebuchadnezzar of Babylon come against Judah and take King Jehoiakim captive to Babylon and set up our current king, Zedekiah, a son of King Josiah, as ruler. Before Nebuchadnezzar returned to Babylon, he took vessels from the Temple and put them in the temple of his god in Babylon. Yet again, it was us, the descendants of Obed-Edom and his clan, that were Temple gatekeepers and Temple storehouse guards, that hid and preserved the Ark of the Covenant, the Golden Lampstand, and the Golden Table of the Presence.

Now, once again, only eleven years later, we of the clan of Obed-Edom find ourselves entrusted with the Ark of the Covenant, the Golden Lampstand, and the Golden Table of the Presence to keep them from being desecrated by invaders. But for these holy items that we have salvaged, Nebuchadnezzar will no doubt take all the remaining vessels of the Temple and the treasures of the Temple storehouse, plus the treasures of the royal treasury, and take them to Babylon to put in the house of his god. Let us acknowledge that King Zedekiah did not honor this Ark of the Covenant as did his ancestors King David and King Solomon or our ancestor Obed-Edom and those of his clan with him. Neither did Zedekiah, his brothers, or his nephew honor the Temple and the things of God. King Josiah, once the law was rediscovered, cleansed the Temple and the land of idols and their priests. Contrarywise, King Zedekiah set up idols in the Temple itself that polluted that holy place. The Shekinah glory of God would not share the Temple with such abominations and departed. King Zedekiah's actions have brought us to this time and place of God's judgment on the Kingdom of Judah, the City of Jerusalem, and the Temple itself.

CHAPTER 9

Where Do We Go Now?

> Turn, O backsliding children, saith the LORD; for I am married unto you: and I will take you one of a city, and two of a family, and I will bring you to Zion: And I will give you pastors according to mine heart, which shall feed you with knowledge and understanding. And it shall come to pass, when ye be multiplied and increased in the land, in those days, saith the LORD, they shall say no more, The Ark of the Covenant of the LORD: neither shall it come to mind: neither shall they remember it; neither shall they visit it; neither shall that be done anymore.
>
> Jeremiah 3:14-16

What Then Shall We Do?

The people gathered around me were silent. Recalling the history of our nation made it abundantly clear how we, as a nation, had been unfaithful to the Lord and brought judgment upon the nation and upon Jerusalem and the Temple. It was a somber thing to take in. However, it was also apparent how our ancestor Obed-Edom and his clan, down to our time, had honored the Lord and His Ark of the Covenant. Their reward, and indeed our reward, was the favor and blessing of God.

My young daughter, Rebecca, rushed over and hugged me tightly around my waist. I embraced her, kissed her forehead, and stroked her long black hair. Then I, Hadar, broke the heavy silence by addressing our company, "Well, my brothers and sisters, what do we do now, and where shall we go? Moreover, what is to become of us? You women, you are free to speak too."

I called out our friend Ebed-Melech and let him know that no one would deny him the opportunity to speak at this time. I went on saying, "The Lord had revealed to the prophet Jeremiah that the time would come when this Ark will not be mentioned, thought about, visited, or another copy made. So I don't think we are to return to Jerusalem. I believe we who have honored the Ark are being given the honor of portering the Ark to whatever place the Lord shall lead us to dwell in."

I added, "Remember also the vision the Lord gave to the prophet Ezekiel, who is already in Babylon with our countrymen that were taken captive eleven years ago by Nebuchadnezzar? The Lord had revealed to Ezekiel that the Shekinah glory of the Lord had already departed from the Ark, the Temple, and from Jerusalem to the nearby mountains and beyond. My brothers, I think we are another fulfillment of the Glory departing. We have portered the Ark of the Covenant from the Temple, from Jerusalem, and to the hills. We have witnessed the miracle of that Glory showing up in this cave and giving us light from the Glory of God that dwells with the Ark of the Covenant. I believe our next move is to be to a place further removed. Just as the book of the law of the Lord was forgotten until it was found in the House of the Lord and read to King Josiah, I believe this Ark of the Covenant is to be forgotten, but this time, it will not return, as the prophet Jeremiah foretold."

The Brass Serpent and the Ark of Gold

I went on to say, "I have been troubled by all of this. Didn't the Lord have the Ark of the Covenant be prepared by Moses as a place of His habitation and to speak in the Tent of Meeting from between the Mercy Seat and the Cherubim? Was not the Ark then portered to the city of David by our ancestor Obed-Edom and our clan and honored by them until and continuing after the Ark was moved to the Temple built by Solomon? Why would it be removed by us not to be seen again?"

We are of the tribe of Levi, and we all study the scriptures and the prophets to get wisdom and understanding. I believe part of the answer we seek lies in another holy thing that the Lord had Moses make in the wilderness when the people were bitten by snakes and died after they murmured against the Lord and against Moses. When the people came to Moses and confessed their sin, God told Moses to make a serpent of brass and put it on a pole. Thereafter, if a person was bitten by a serpent, he only had to look on the serpent of brass, and he lived. Many years later, under King Hezekiah's reign, who did what was right in the sight of the Lord, he destroyed idols from among the people. He also broke into pieces the serpent of brass that Moses had made because the people had been burning incense to it and called it Nehushtan.

Transition from One Covenant
to a Better Covenant

My brothers and sisters, I believe the Lord is removing the Ark of the Covenant, and preserving our lives in the process, because He is preparing another better covenant such that the Ark, representing the old covenant that we have known, will not be remembered. Moses gave us the words of the Lord when he said, "The LORD our God would raise up a prophet from us like Moses himself, and we should listen to that prophet because God's words will be in his mouth." Now in times past, God spoke from the Mercy Seat of the Ark of the Covenant between the Cherubim. But I see a new covenant where God will speak to us from this future prophet Moses spoke about. Did not King David write in his Psalms, "The LORD said to me, You are My Son; I have begotten You this day?" Apparently, the Lord is sending, in His own good time, someone who is greater than this Ark, as hard as that is for us to imagine. The old must give way to the new and better.

I added, "Elsewhere in the Book of the Law and the scrolls of the prophets, the Lord has spoken of this change. This golden Ark of the Covenant was commissioned by God, but fabricated by human hands. There is coming a living Ark to represent the pact between God and His people. The prophet Isaiah prophesied, 'To us, a child is born, to us, a son is given: and the government will be upon his shoulder: and his name shall be called Wonderful Counselor, The Mighty God, The everlasting Father, The Prince of Peace.' Again, in another place, Isaiah said, 'Arise and shine; for your light has come, and the Glory of the Lord is risen upon you–the Lord will arise upon you, and His Glory shall be seen upon you. And the heathen will come to your light, and kings to the brightness of your rising.'"

When our ancestor Jacob blessed and prophesied over his sons just before his death, upon coming to Judah, he said, "The scepter will not depart from Judah, nor a lawgiver from between his feet, until Shiloh come; and to him will the people gather and give heed in obedience." Now Joshua, after the conquest of Canaan, set up the Ark of the Covenant in Shiloh where the people went to worship and offer sacrifices. In our Hebrew language, Shiloh means he who is to be sent. So, Jacob was not speaking prophetically of a place but of a descendant of Judah. Surely, this ruler to come will also be a descendant in the line of King David. Of this man to come, the prophet Isaiah said, "The LORD has laid on him the iniquity of us all." Isaiah went on to say, "God will make his soul an offering for sin," adding, "my righteous servant will justify many; for he will bear their iniquities."

I added, "The prophet Jeremiah also confirmed the prophecy of Isaiah. Speaking by the Lord, Jeremiah said, 'The days are coming that I will raise up a righteous branch, a descendant of David. As a King, he will reign and prosper.' Jeremiah went on to say, 'This is the name by which he shall be called, *the Lord our righteousness.*'"

Brothers and sisters, before the Spirit departed, as the Lord revealed to the prophet Ezekiel, this Ark produced its own light from the Glory of the Lord. There was no candlestick in the Most Holy Place in the Temple where the Ark resided because man-made light was not necessary. The Glory of God from His Presence provided light. This one who is to come, Shiloh, is from God Himself, and the Glory of the Lord will be upon him and in him. The prophet Habakkuk, speaking of him, said, "His brightness was as the light; he had beams of light coming out of his hands, and it was there that his power was hidden." In the Psalms, it is written, "You did not desire sacrifices and offerings—you did not require burnt offerings and sin offerings. Then I said, look, I am coming; in the volume of the book, it is me that it was written about."

When God tested Abraham and instructed him to offer his son Isaac as a burnt offering, Abraham told his son, Isaac, "God will provide Himself a lamb" for the sacrifice. When God saw that Abraham would not withhold his own son, the Angel of the Lord prevented Abraham from harming the lad, and Abraham found a ram caught in a thicket that he offered up, but the lamb is yet to come, it is from God, and it will not be an animal. This lamb is the one spoken of in scripture as Shiloh and will be God's own Son.

In the Ark of the Covenant, the law is engraved by the finger of God on the stone tablets, and above them is the Mercy Seat. As told in the Psalms, "Mercy and truth meet together; righteousness and peace embrace and kiss each other." In the Ark of the Covenant, which we have with us in this cave, we see how the Lord our God is true to the justice of the law, His commandments, and His holy righteousness, and yet by His mercy and a blood sacrifice, we are redeemed from the curse of the law. Jerusalem may never see this golden Ark again, but a new and better living Ark of a new covenant is coming. God will require the just punishment of our sins, but in His mercy, He will provide His lamb to take away our sins and redeem us to fellowship with our God. In another place, the prophet Isaiah, speaking God's words, said, "Look, I Am doing a new thing! It is springing up; don't you see it?" We have been chosen to witness the beginning of this new thing.

This golden Ark of the Covenant has been with us since the time of Moses, but it must fade from memory and be forgotten to make way for Shiloh, who is to come. Unlike the serpent of brass, this Ark will not overstay its time and allow wicked, unfaithful priests to make it an idol that must be destroyed, as King Hezekiah broke the brass serpent into pieces when it was polluted from its original purpose. I don't know when the new thing will come bringing in the new covenant, but I am determined that we, as the descendants of Obed-Edom and his clan, will be faithful servants of the will of God in this our time.

As we wait in this cave, the people of Jerusalem are about to be slaughtered, and the Temple and city walls burnt and broken down. Those that remain will be taken captive to Babylon. Yet, the prophets have spoken of a time when the Kingdoms of Judah and Israel will return to the land and be one nation. At that time, the throne of God will be among us, and we will serve him and not stray to serve the idols and false gods of the nations. At that time, this Ark we honor will have no place, nor will it be remembered.

Again, the prophet Isaiah spoke by the Lord, saying, "Look, I am creating new heavens and a new earth: and the former won't be remembered anymore, nor will it come to mind." Once more, Isaiah spoke forth the words of the Lord, saying, "Don't even think about the former things, nor consider the things of olden times." Finally, our prophet Jeremiah, who has charged us with this mission, said, "Behold, the days are coming, says the LORD, when I will make a new covenant with the house of Israel and the house of Judah—not according to the covenant that I made with their fathers when I took them by the hand to lead them out of the land of Egypt."

At this time, Ebed-Melech spoke up, saying, "Hadar, my friend, we cannot remain here. When the opportunity comes, let us leave this place. If you all agree, I will lead this company to Egypt and from there to my native Ethiopia. There we can wait in safety to see how the Lord will lead us. In the meantime, you men of the clan of Obed-Edom who have continued to honor and guard the Ark of the Covenant can continue to do so as it pleases the Lord God, together with your wives and children."

This seemed well to us. So we determined to do as suggested by Ebed-Melech. Even so, our hearts were breaking because of the massacre of those in Jerusalem, the breaking down of the walls of that great city, and the burning and destruction of the Temple. It brought to mind the travail of a woman in childbirth. In that case, there is much pain before something new comes into being.

EPILOGUE

Or have ye not read in the law, how that on the sabbath days the priests in the temple profane the sabbath, and are blameless? But I say unto you, That in this place is one greater than the temple. But if ye had known what this meaneth, I will have mercy, and not sacrifice, ye would not have condemned the guiltless.

For the Son of man is Lord even of the sabbath day.

Matthew 12:5-8

Likewise also the cup after supper, saying, This cup is the new testament in my blood, which is shed for you.

Luke 22:20

And the Word was made flesh, and dwelt among us, (and we beheld his Glory, the Glory as of the only begotten of the Father,) full of grace and truth.

John 1:14

The coming of God in flesh, born of a virgin, marked the new thing. Jesus the Christ established a new covenant in His blood and by being a willing sacrifice in crucifixion on a cross on a hill called the place of the skull overlooking Jerusalem. He is why there is a New Testament section of the Holy Bible. He could rightly say that He was greater than the Temple. He was also greater than the Golden Ark of the Covenant, which was not in the Temple of His day, nor did anyone speak about it. The descendants of Obed-Edom removed it centuries earlier lest it fall into the hands of the Chaldeans, but also to make way for the transition to the one who is greater than the Ark of the Covenant. They were fulfilling prophesy. It is my sincere prayer that you, the reader, like Obed-Edom and his descendants, would choose the Glory. Choose Jesus Christ, our God and Savior. Be willing to forsake other things in order to gain the Glory and walk out the prophecy spoken and written to cover the destiny of your own life.

ABOUT THE AUTHOR

Louis McCall was born in Chicago, Illinois, and attended Northwestern University, where he received a PhD in political science. Later, he also attended the National War College of the National Defense University. Louis was an Assistant Professor at the Ohio State University in the Department of Political Science prior to a thirty-six-year career in the US Department of State, first as a Foreign Service officer and then as a foreign affairs Civil Service employee where he served as Consul General in Florence, Italy, Chargé d'Affaires in Brunei, US Representative to the Republic of San Marino, and Assistant Inspector General.

He lived in or worked in, at least temporarily, more than sixty countries on six continents. Whether in academia or as a diplomat, Louis found opportunities to live his faith, including part-time ministry of the good news in word and in song, including co-laboring with missionaries, national church leaders, and the underground church. When ministering early in his diplomatic career from the pulpit of a great church in Calcutta, India, Louis said to those in attendance that he had determined not to be ashamed of the gospel of Christ. That has been a commitment he has endeavored to keep over the years. In his final two years at the Department of State, he organized and led the National Day of Prayer observances in the Department.

Now, in his new career as an author, he has the pleasure of greater freedom in sharing what God has placed in his heart. Louis is active simultaneously in two churches in Washington, DC. One is a multi-site non-denominational church, and the other a Catholic church where he is a regular cantor, though not a Catholic himself. He has managed this with the blessing and full knowledge of pastors and priests. This has been an outgrowth of his early association with a mixed protestant-Catholic charismatic house-based worship group, his association with the late Saint Mother Teresa of Calcutta, his charismatic Catholic wife, Lenora, and guest ministry in churches and Bible schools of various denominations while living in or working in other countries.

Louis is the author of *According to Your Word Lord, I Pray* and of *The Epic of God*.

To Contact or Follow the Author

I truly hope you enjoyed this book. It was written for you. Please recommend it to others. I also welcome your feedback. It would really encourage me to hear from you. You can follow me on my website and on social media using the links below.

Website: http://www.louismccallinternational.com

Address: Louis McCall International PO Box 60211 Washington, DC 20039

Twitter: @DrLouisMcCall